GALE
CENGAGE Learning

Short Stories for Students, Volume 37

Project Editor: Matthew Derda

Rights Acquisition and Management: Christine Myaskovsky, Robin Young Composition: Evi Abou-El-Seoud Manufacturing: Rhonda A. Dover Imaging: John Watkins

Product Design: Pamela A. E. Galbreath, Jennifer Wahi Digital Content Production: Allie Semperger Product Manager: Meggin Condino © 2013 Gale, Cengage Learning

For product information and technology assistance, contact us at **Gale Customer Support, 1-800-877-4253.**

For permission to use material from this text or product, submit all requests online at **www.cengage.com/permissions**.

Further permissions questions can be emailed to **permissionrequest@cengage.com** While every effort has been made to ensure the reliability of the information presented in this publication, Gale, a part of Cengage Learning, does not guarantee the accuracy of the data contained herein. Gale accepts no payment for listing; and inclusion in the publication of any organization, agency, institution, publication, service, or individual does not imply endorsement of the editors or publisher. Errors brought to the attention of the publisher and verified to the satisfaction of the publisher will be corrected in future editions.

Gale
27500 Drake Rd.
Farmington Hills, MI, 48331-3535

ISBN-13: 978-1-4144-8742-7
ISBN-10: 1-4144-8742-8
ISSN 1092-7735

This title is also available as an e-book.

ISBN-13: 978-1-4144-8759-5
ISBN-10: 1-4144-8759-2
Contact your Gale, a part of Cengage Learning sales
representative for ordering information.

Printed in Mexico
1 2 3 4 5 6 7 17 16 15 14 13

Interpreter of Maladies

Jhumpa Lahiri 1999

Introduction

"Interpreter of Maladies" is a short story by Jhumpa Lahiri, an American writer of Indian descent. It was first published in 1998 in *Agni Review* and then reprinted in 1999 as the title story in the author's first short-story collection, which was awarded the Pulitzer Prize. "Interpreter of Maladies" received the O. Henry Award and was included in the 1999 edition of *Best American Short Stories.* The story is about the Das family, an American family of Indian descent who are on a trip to India to visit relatives. They hire an Indian tour guide who takes them by car to visit places of interest to tourists. The guide, Mr. Kapasi, also works as an interpreter for a doctor, some of whose patients speak a language the doctor does not understand. During the trip, Mrs. Das, who is unhappily married, confesses to Mr. Kapasi a secret from her past that is tormenting her, hoping that he will be able to offer a cure for her malady.

Lahiri explained in an interview for the Houghton Mifflin Harcourt website that she first had the idea for the story in 1991, when she was a graduate student at Boston University. An acquaintance of hers was working as an interpreter for a doctor who had Russian patients who did not speak English. Lahiri decided that one day she would write a story titled "interpreter of maladies." It was not until five years later, however, that the basic outline of the story came to her. When she was putting together her first short-story collection, she knew that "Interpreter of Maladies" had to be the title story of the collection "because it best expresses, thematically, the predicament at the heart of the book—the dilemma, the difficulty, and often the impossibility of communicating emotional pain and affliction to others, as well as expressing it to ourselves."

Nilanjana Sudeshna Lahiri was born to Indian parents in London, England, on July 11, 1967. When she was three, the family immigrated to the United States, and Lahiri was raised in South Kingston, Rhode Island. Her father was a librarian at the University of Rhode Island, and her mother was a schoolteacher.

Although they lived in the United States, Lahiri's parents considered themselves Indian, and every few years they made trips to Calcutta, accompanied by their two daughters. Lahiri would stay in India for periods lasting up to six months, although she did not feel at home there. Nor did she feel quite at home in Rhode Island, where she was conscious of her different ethnic background and often felt like an outsider.

Lahiri became an avid reader when she was a child, and she also began to write stories. At the age of seven, she would coauthor with her classmates stories of up to ten pages in length. The first name by which she became known, Jhumpa, was a nick name bestowed on her by a teacher in elementary school.

She attended South Kingstown High School and then Barnard College, from which she received a bachelor of arts degree in English literature in 1989. Continuing her studies, she received three master of arts degrees from Boston University, in

English, creative writing, and comparative literature and the arts. She also obtained a doctoral degree in Renaissance studies from the same university. While still a graduate student, Lahiri had already begun writing short stories and had won the Henfield Prize from *Transatlantic Review* in 1993 and the *Louisville Review* fiction prize in 1997.

Lahiri taught creative writing at Boston University and the Rhode Island School of Design, but her goal was to write fiction. Her breakthrough occurred when the *New Yorker* published three of her stories and named her one of the twenty best young writers in the United States. Her collection of nine short stories, *Interpreter of Maladies,* which includes the story of the same name, was published in 1999. It won the Pulitzer Prize for Fiction in 2000. The title story was awarded the O. Henry Award in 1999.

In 2003, Lahiri's first novel, *The Namesake* was published. The novel is about a family that moves from Calcutta to New York. One of the main characters is a second-generation Indian American named Gogol, who struggles to find his place in the world. The novel was nominated for the 2003 *Los Angeles Times* book award for fiction. It was made into a movie directed by Mira Nair. Lahiri's second short-story collection, *Unaccustomed Earth,* appeared in 2008. It won the Frank O'Connor International Short Story Award in 2008 and an Asian American Literary Award in 2009.

Lahiri married Alberto Vourvoulias, an American-born journalist, in 2001. They have two children, Octavio (b. 2002) and Noor (b. 2005). As of 2012, they live in Brooklyn, New York.

Plot Summary

As "Interpreter of Maladies" begins, Mr. and Mrs. Das are visiting India to see their parents. The couple are of Indian descent, but they were born in the United States and live in New Brunswick, New Jersey. They dress and talk like Americans. They are accompanied by their three young children, Tina, Robby, and Bobby. On the day the story takes place, the family is on a sightseeing trip, and they have hired a tour guide, the middle-aged Mr. Kapasi, who is driving them to see the Sun Temple at Konarak. It is a two-and-a-half hour journey by car. The children are excited by the monkeys they see in the trees that line the road. They have never seen monkeys outside of a zoo before. Mr. Das asks the guide to stop the car so he can take a photograph. Shortly afterward, they stop again so Mr. Das can take a picture of an emaciated man sitting on top of a cart of grain sacks.

As the American couple converses with Mr. Kapasi, he tells them some details about his life. He works as an interpreter for a doctor. Mr. Kapasi speaks Gujarati, a language that the doctor does not understand but that is spoken by many of his patients. Mrs. Das shows some interest in this and gets him to talk more about it. Mr. Kapasi gives an example of a patient who had a pain in his throat. After Mr. Kapasi translated the man's description of his symptoms, the doctor was able to prescribe the correct medicine. Mr. and Mrs. Das agree that the interpreter has a big responsibility in these situations. The patients depend on his translations being accurate. For his part, however, Mr. Kapasi does not like his job. In his youth he had wanted to become an interpreter for diplomats and world leaders, helping to settle disputes between nations. But his dreams were never realized. He had taught English in a grammar school, but then his son had contracted a fatal illness, and he had taken the job with the doctor because it was better paid, and he needed money to pay all the medical bills.

Mr. Kapasi is flattered by the interest Mrs. Das shows in him, which contrasts with the indifference he experiences from his wife. He tells her about more of the patients whose symptoms he has translated to the doctor. She listens attentively.

They stop at a restaurant for lunch, and Mrs. Das asks Mr. Kapasi for his address, so they can send him copies of the photographs Mr. Das has been taking. Mr. Kapasi writes his address down on a piece of paper and gives it to her. He allows himself to hope they will correspond with each other, confide in each other, and become good friends.

In the afternoon, they reach the Sun Temple, which was built in the thirteenth century. As they examine it, Mr. Das reads aloud details from a guidebook. The whole family enjoys seeing the temple, which pleases Mr. Kapasi. He is especially pleased that Mrs. Das seems interested in the temple. He likes her because she has taken an interest in him. He wants to be alone with her so they can continue their conversation. She inquires about one of the bronze sculptures of Surya, the sun god, and he is able to answer her. He looks forward to the correspondence he anticipates that they will have, in which they will explain things about their respective countries to each other. This will, he thinks, in a way fulfill his dream of being an interpreter between nations.

After two hours, Mr. Kapasi starts to drive the family back to their hotel. But he is reluctant to see them go, so he suggests visiting another tourist destination, where monastic dwellings were carved out of the hillsides.

When they arrive there, Mrs. Das says she is tired and will remain in the car. Mr. Das takes the children up to the hills, while Mrs. Das talks to Mr. Kapasi. He is surprised to hear her confess that one of her sons, Bobby, is not her husband's son. Her husband does not know this, however, since Mrs. Das has kept it secret from him for eight years. Mr. Kapasi is the first person she has told.

Mrs. Das goes on to tell Mr. Kapasi the story of her marriage. She had known Raj Das since they were children, and they married young. She got lonely staying at home raising their children while her husband worked as a schoolteacher. When a friend of Raj Das's came to stay with them for a week because he had job interviews in the area, Mina Das allowed herself to be seduced by him. The friend later married, and the two couples stay in touch, but Mrs. Das never informed the man that he was Bobby's father. She tells Mr. Kapasi that she feels terrible about this, and she hopes he can offer her some advice. She wants him to say something that will make her feel better.

Unfortunately, Mr. Kapasi feels depressed by her story. He even feels insulted that she should seek his assistance. Nonetheless, he decides it is his duty to help her. He thinks he may advise her to confess the truth to her husband. Then perhaps he, Mr. Kapasi, could act as a mediator. He begins by asking her whether what she feels is really pain, or is it guilt? She appears displeased by the question and declines to answer it. Without uttering a word, she gets out of the car and begins to walk up the path. She eats some puffed rice, but it keeps falling through her fingers, and soon there are half a dozen monkeys following her, eating the rice that falls. Mr. Kapasi gets out of the car and follows her, trying to scare the monkeys away.

Mrs. Das joins her family, where Mr. Das is preparing to take a family photo. Then they realize that Bobby is missing. They search for him, to find him crying and terrified, surrounded by about a dozen monkeys who are pulling at his tee shirt. Puffed rice is on the ground, and one monkey has been beating him about the legs with a stick. Mrs. Das appeals to Mr. Kapasi for help. Mr. Kapasi manages to drive the monkeys away with a fallen tree branch. He picks Bobby up and carries him to his parents. Bobby has not suffered any serious harm. They all agree that they should return immediately to the hotel. Mrs. Das reaches into her bag for a hairbrush, and as she pulls it out, the piece of paper on which Mr. Kapasi wrote his address comes out too, and it flutters away in the breeze, eventually coming to rest in the trees with the monkeys. No one but Mr. Kapasi notices.

Characters

Bobby

Bobby is close in age to Ronny and is being raised as the son of Mr. and Mrs. Das. In fact, Mr. Das is not his father. His father is a friend of Mr. Das's who stayed for a week at their house in New Brunswick, New Jersey, while he was interviewing for jobs in the area. Bobby does not know this and thinks Mr. Das is his father. In the story, Bobby gets separated from the family as they visit the hills and is attacked by a group of monkeys. He is not seriously injured.

Mrs. Mina Das

Mrs. Das is twenty-eight years old, the mother of three small children. Like her husband, she is of Indian heritage but was born in the United States and has lived there all her life. On the car journey to the Sun Temple, she gives the impression of being bored, and she does not interact in any meaningful way with her young daughter, even though the girl seeks her mother's attention. Nor does Mrs. Das communicate much with her husband, other than to complain that he failed to rent an air-conditioned car just because he wanted to save a small amount of money. Mrs. Das does, however, take an interest in Mr. Kapasi, asking him questions about his job and complimenting him about it. Later, she talks to

Mr. Kapasi in a surprisingly personal way, telling him the history of her marriage. She had married while still in college and quickly gave birth to a son. But she had been overwhelmed by the responsibility of raising a child. She did not have a wide social circle, and her friends gradually fell away, leaving her feeling isolated as she stayed at home all day looking after the child. She was always tired.

Mrs. Das even tells Mr. Kapasi a secret that she has kept from her husband: Mr. Das is not the father of her son Bobby. The boy was fathered by a friend of her husband's during the time he was staying at their house in New Jersey. Mrs. Das is distressed by having to carry this secret. She has told no one of it, and Bobby is now eight years old. She turns to Mr. Kapasi, hoping that he can say something that will ease her pain, but she is disappointed in his response. For his part, her revelation dampens his interest in her, and he is unable to console her.

Mr. Raj Das

Mr. Das was born in America to Indian parents. Raised in America, he teaches science at a middle school in New Brunswick, New Jersey. Now in his late twenties, he is returning to India with his wife to visit their retired parents. Everything about Mr. Das, from his firm handshake to the way he speaks and dresses, marks him as an American. Despite his heritage, he knows little of India.

He and Mrs. Das are not especially happy

together and bicker a lot. They have been married for more than eight years and were both still in college when they married. Mr. Das is not very perceptive in his emotional life. He does not realize that over the years his wife has ceased to be able to talk to him about anything important. Mrs. Das tells Mr. Kapasi that her husband thinks she is still in love with him.

Mr. Das has a relaxed parenting style, not imposing much discipline on his children. During the car trip, he seems more interested in his guidebook than in his family. One of his hobbies appears to be photography, since he has an expensive camera and takes a lot of photographs of the family and the places they visit. He wants to take a photo including all the family that he can use on their Christmas cards. It appears that he likes to maintain the image of a happy family and is ignorant of the fissures within it, including his wife's estrangement and the fact that the younger son, Bobby, is not in fact his biological son.

Mr. Kapasi

Mr. Kapasi is a neatly dressed Indian man in his midforties. He has two occupations. His main job is working as an interpreter for a doctor who does not speak the language that many of his patients speak. Mr. Kapasi translates their descriptions of their symptoms so that the doctor can prescribe the correct treatment. Two days a week, Mr. Kapasi works as a tour guide, driving tourists to local places of interest. When he was young, Mr. Kapasi had a more ambitious dream of how his life would turn out. He wanted to be a high-level interpreter, working for governments, helping to solve problems between nations. He is a self-taught man who learned several languages. However, opportunity did not come his way. Instead, when he was younger he worked as an English teacher in a grammar school. Then his seven-year-old son contracted a fatal illness and he took the job as interpreter, which paid twice as much as the teaching position, so he could pay the medical bills. In spite of the adequate salary, however, it is not a job he likes or feels proud of. For him, it is a sign of his failure.

Mr. Kapasi, who has several children other than the boy who died, is unhappily married. He and his wife have nothing in common other than their children. She does not support his career and refers to him not as an interpreter but as a "doctor's assistant," a term he finds demeaning. He thinks that his occupation merely reminds his wife of the son they lost.

Given his own dissatisfaction with his life, it is perhaps not surprising that Mr. Kapasi is flattered by the interest Mrs. Das takes in his occupation. She seems to respect him for it, commenting that he has a big responsibility. She even calls his work "romantic." Mr. Kapasi finds himself thinking about her in a mildly erotic way, and he also allows himself to entertain a daydream about becoming friends with her through the exchange of letters. But when she makes her confession to him about her act of adultery, he does not receive it well, feeling insulted that she should expect him to give her advice on such a matter.

Ronny

Ronny is the older son of Mr. and Mrs. Das. He is about nine years old.

Tina

Tina is the young daughter of Mr. and Mrs. Das. She is on her first trip to India. Her mother does not pay much attention to her needs.

Themes

Communication

The theme of communication is conveyed in several ways in Lahiri's story. Mr. Kapasi's job as a translator for a doctor involves communication. He acts as an intermediary between two people, doctor and patient, who would otherwise be unable to communicate at all because of language differences. His work as a translator demands accuracy, and the communication he facilitates allows the doctor to heal his patients. This smooth form of communication that Mr. Kapasi helps to facilitate in his occupation stands in contrast to the breakdown in communication between people that characterizes much of the story. This applies especially to the two central characters, Mr. Kapasi and Mrs. Das, both of whom suffer from emotional isolation. During the course of the story they both try to break out of their isolation in ways that are ill-thought out and that do not produce the results they had hoped for.

What Mr. Kapasi and Mrs. Das have in common is an unhappy marriage. Mr. Kapasi and his wife do not communicate much, and she has no respect for his job of interpreter. He regards himself and his wife as a "bad match." They are two people formally joined together by marriage but with little in common. When he observes "the bickering, the indifference, the protracted silences" between Mr.

and Mrs. Das, he recognizes it as similar to what he experiences in his own marriage.

Because of their unhappy marriages, both Mr. Kapasi and Mrs. Das feel somewhat isolated. Mr. Kapasi has a deep desire to connect with someone more closely. It is because of this that he gets carried away when Mrs. Das shows some polite interest in his work and asks for his address so she can send him a copy of the photograph her husband took of them sitting together. Mr. Kapasi imagines corresponding with Mrs. Das, building up a friendship, sharing details of their lives in a way that neither is able to do in their respective marriages. He even compares the feeling he gets from imagining this to the pleasure he used to experience when he was learning to translate from French or Italian. Communication, crossing the differences between languages and between people, seems to be something that Mr. Kapasi values very deeply. He has a momentary desire to embrace Mrs. Das, "to freeze with her, even for an instant," but of course this is an act of intimacy that can never occur. The impossibility of it is shown symbolically at the end, when the piece of paper on which Mr. Kapasi has written his address escapes from Mrs. Das's bag, blows away, and nestles high in the trees.

Similarly, Mrs. Das makes an attempt at communicating with Mr. Kapasi, not for the sake of establishing a friendship with him, but simply to unburden herself of a dark secret that she has been carrying around for eight years. She confesses to Mr. Kapasi that her son Bobby was fathered not by her husband but by her husband's friend, and she goes on to tell the surprised tour guide the story of her unhappy marriage. It is ironic that she is able to confide in a stranger but not in her own husband. Her demand that Mr. Kapasi produce some balm for her malady is unrealistic. Trapped in her emotional isolation, she has no sensible plan for how to break out of it since the lack of communication between herself and her husband has become almost absolute. The story thus shows how difficult it is to escape from the prison of isolation. Both of these characters seize on what they think is an opportunity to do so, but neither ends up any better off than when they started.

Topics for Further Study

- Read another story by Lahiri in the collection *Interpreter of Maladies* and write an essay in which you compare and contrast it with

"Interpreter of Maladies." What themes are common to both stories?

- Using the Internet, research the topic of second-generation South Asian Americans. Do they tend to identify entirely with the American culture, or do they also try to preserve their South Asian heritage? How does their experience in the United States resemble or differ from that of other immigrant groups? Make a class presentation in which you discuss your research.

- Consult *Talk: Teen Art of Communication* (2006), by Dale Carlson and Kishore Khairnar, a book for teens that offers practical advice about how to communicate effectively with the different people they know. Take some of the examples in the book and practice with a partner the art of communication. One suggestion: Read pages 60–62, about the need to listen without judging or interpreting. Find a partner. One person then talks for a couple of minutes about some emotional issue he or she is dealing with. The other person listens without interrupting and then takes a minute to speak back to the first person what he or she has just said, without judging, commenting, or interpreting.

- Imagine that "Interpreter of Maladies" is being made into a movie. Go to Glogster. com and create an interactive poster to advertise the movie version. Link it to your Facebook or Twitter page so all your friends can see and comment on it.

Responsibility

Mr. and Mrs. Das, as seen through the eyes of Mr. Kapasi, are presented as not being very mature or responsible. When he first sees them, Mr. Kapasi is struck by how young they look. The narrator comments that Mr. Das's voice, "somehow tentative and a little shrill, sounded as though it had not yet settled into maturity." Mr. Das observes that the couple does not act like parents. They do not supervise their children very closely. When Tina plays with the lock in the car, for example, Mrs. Das does nothing to stop her. The parents' joint failure to supervise Bobby leads to the attack on him by the monkeys. Nor do the parents discipline the children. When Bobby shows no inclination to obey an instruction from his father, Mr. Das does nothing about it. Mr. Kapasi thinks they are not responsible parents. He observes that Mr. and Mrs. Das "behaved like an older brother and sister, not parents. It seemed that they were in charge of the children only for the day; it was hard to believe they were regularly responsible for anything other than themselves." The lack of responsibility is also shown in Mrs. Das's act of marital infidelity and the secret she keeps from both father and son. It appears that she has been so overwhelmed by her responsibilities as mother and wife that she has developed a habit of ignoring them that she cannot now break. "She was lost behind her sunglasses," Mr. Kapasi observes, and she walks past her children "as if they were strangers."

Point of View

The story is told by a limited third-person narrator from the point of view of Mr. Kapasi. This means that the narrator has insight only into the thoughts and feelings of Mr. Kapasi. The other characters are seen through his eyes. In other words, the reader gets to know Mr. and Mrs. Das by means of the impressions they make on Mr. Kapasi and the ideas he forms of them, in addition to their actions and the things they say directly.

Imagery and Symbolism

Mr. Das is not as central to the story as his wife and Mr. Kapasi, but he is neatly characterized by the author with the help of a recurring image, that of the camera. Mr. and Mrs. Das, it must be remembered, do not have a happy marriage, but Mrs. Das tells Mr. Kapasi that she thinks her husband still believes that she loves him. Mr. Das is therefore ignorant of his wife's true feelings as well as being completely unaware that one of the boys he has raised as his son is not his biological son. Mr. Das is seen often with his expensive high-tech camera, snapping photographs of the local sites and of his family. He knows how to look at things from the outside, but he seems oblivious to the inner condition of his marriage. Shortly after Mrs. Das has explained her unhappiness to Mr. Kapasi, Mr. Das is shown wanting to get yet another shot of the entire family. He wants to use it for their Christmas cards that year. His photos may appear to show a happy, intact family, but the reality is rather different, and the reader gets a keen sense of the irony of the situation.

Mrs. Das is presented as being careless and irresponsible, and this is symbolized by the trail of puffed rice that she spills as she walks to rejoin her family after making her confession to Mr. Kapasi. She is unaware that as she eats the rice, chunks of it fall to the ground. It is this trail of puffed rice that causes the crisis in which the monkeys attack Bobby. Mrs. Das's untidiness, her failure to exert self-control, is symbolic of her conduct in her marriage.

Another image is that of the wild, unruly monkeys. They might perhaps be seen as symbolic of the turbulent emotions that are felt by the two central characters but are not expressed—or at least, in Mrs. Das's case, not expressed to the right person. Both these characters keep up a surface appearance that is not related to their inner dissatisfaction.

Indian Immigration and Cultural Assimilation

"Interpreter of Maladies" illustrates the interaction of two cultures, American and Indian. Although both Mr. and Mrs. Das have Indian parents, they were born and raised in the United States and dress and behave as Americans. They do not speak Indian languages, and in India they act like tourists rather than Indian people returning home. This aspect of the story illustrates the theme of immigration and cultural assimilation. Mr. and Mrs. Das are second-generation immigrants. Usually, people in that category either experience some conflict about their cultural identity or identify with the only country they have known. First-generation immigrants tend to identify more with the culture of their homeland. This appears to have been the case with the parents of Mr. and Mrs. Das, who have returned to India rather than continue to live in the United States.

Compare & Contrast

- **1990s:** According to the 2000 Census, the Indian American community in the United States numbers 1,678,765. It is the third-largest Asian community after Chinese Americans and Filipino Americans. The numbers are growing rapidly, with an increase of 106 percent from 1990 to 2000.

Today: According to the 2010 Census, there are 2,846,914 Indian Americans living in the United States. The average annual growth rate for the Indian American community is 10.5 percent.

- **1990s:** The Indian American community shows high levels of educational attainment. Some 58 percent of Indian Americans have received a bachelor's degree or higher, compared with only 20 percent of the US population as a whole. Indian Americans are also successful in their careers. Nearly 44 percent of those in the workforce are in managerial or specialist positions. Over 5,000 Indian Americans teach in US colleges; 30,000 Indian American doctors practice in the United States.

Today: Indian Americans are among the most successful and prosperous of immigrant groups in the United States. Nearly 67 percent hold bachelor's or higher degrees. About 77 percent hold a professional position. Median income for Indian

American families is $69,470, as compared to $38,885 for all American families. There are 200,000 Indian American millionaires.

- **1990s:** According to the 2000 Census, the largest Indian American populations are in California (314,819), New York (251,724), New Jersey (169,180), Texas (129,365), Illinois (124,723), and Florida (70,740).

  Today: According to the 2010 Census, the largest Indian American populations are in California (528,176), New York (313,620), New Jersey (292,256), Texas (245,981), Illinois (188,328), and Florida (128,735).

The interaction of these two cultures, Indian and American, is a theme in many of Lahiri's stories. Lahiri was raised in the United States by Indian immigrant parents who still identified with their country of origin. She therefore understood the experience of the Indian immigrant in America. The Indian American community grew considerably during the latter years of the twentieth century, following the 1965 Immigration and Naturalization Act. This act removed the national origins quota system in favor of criteria that emphasized possession of desirable skills. In the story it was probably around this time that the parents of Mr. and Mrs. Das came to the United States, and Mina Das and Raj Das would have been born around the early 1970s.

During the 1970s, large Indian American communities developed in the United States, mainly in four states, California, New York, New Jersey (where Mr. and Mrs. Das are from), and Texas. Indian immigrants on the whole adjusted quickly to life in the United States, and they became one of the most prosperous of immigrant groups. Many became highly paid professionals such as doctors. During the 1980s, the Indian American community became more diverse, as those who were already in the United States sponsored their relatives to join them. In the 1990s, Indian immigrants made significant contributions to the booming information technology industry. Many Indian entrepreneurs settled in California's Silicon Valley and established their own successful high-tech companies there.

Indian Literature in English

Coinciding with the increase of Indian immigration to the United States has been the growth of literature written by Indians in English. In addition to Lahiri, Indian writers who have settled in the United States, such as Bharati Mukherjee, have taken as their subject matter the collective experience of Indian immigrants in North America. With *Interpreter of Maladies,* then, Lahiri was contributing to a growing body of work by Indians or those of Indian heritage living in the West.

During the 1990s, when Lahiri was writing the stories in *Interpreter of Maladies,* several other new writers of Indian origin made their mark. Vikram Seth is known for his novel *A Suitable Boy* (1993). Kiran Desai, a permanent resident of the United States who was born in India, published her well-received first novel, *Hullabaloo in the Guava Orchard*, in 1998. She is the daughter of Anita Desai, also a noted Indian author. Vikram Chandra, also born in India, received widespread recognition when he published his first novel, *Red Earth and Pouring Rain: A Novel,* in 1995 and the five stories that make up his collection *Love and Longing in Bombay* (1997). Pankaj Mishra's novel *The Romantics* (1999), set in India, deals with the clash between Eastern and Western culture. The novel won the Los Angeles Times Art Seidenbaum Award for First Fiction.

Critical Overview

As the title story in a Pulitzer Prize–winning collection, "Interpreter of Maladies" attracted the attention of literary critics. In his essay "Jhumpa Lahiri: *Interpreter of Maladies* (2000)," Paul Brians states that the story is "of two people crossing at an angle through each other's lives, neither satisfied with the response of the other." He notes also that "Lahiri skillfully builds the tension as we gradually realize how much Mr. Kapasi desires Mrs. Das, and how much he has let his fantasies carry him away in dreams of a romantic future." Noelle Brada-Williams, in "Reading Jhumpa Lahiri's *Interpreter of Maladies* as a Short Story Cycle," notes the contrast between the characterization of Mrs. Das and that of Mr. Kapasi. The latter takes care with everything, from his appearance to his manners and his occupation, and he takes his responsibilities seriously. Mrs. Das, however, does not. This contrast between the two, according to Brada-Williams,

> makes their final disconnect inevitable. While they both can be seen longing for communication with others, Mrs. Das is a woman with a life of relative comfort and ease who yearns to be freed of the responsibilities of marriage and children, and Mr. Kapasi is a man who has given up his dreams to

support his family and who only yearns for some recognition and interest in his life.

Not every critic has seen the story in entirely positive terms. In the *Dictionary of Literary Biography*, Rezaul Karim remarks that the style is "marked by occasional overwriting, excessive symbolism, unnatural dialogue, an ironic tone, and some editorializing." According to Karim, the story reveals the Das family's "attitude to India as one of snobbish distance and their interest in India as tourists's interest." For Purvi Shah, reviewing the story in *Amerasia Journal*, the story is "well-crafted, like all of Lahiri's stories. But the writing, as in other pieces in the collection, feels like material produced for a writing workshop—too belabored and mechanical."

What Do I Read Next?

- Unaccustomed Earth (2008) is

Lahiri's second collection of short stories. These eight stories, like those in Interpreter of Maladies, deal with families of Indian heritage and show how they are adjusting across generations to the experience of immigration to the United States. Lahiri examines with an acute eye for telling detail the forces that shape and challenge such families and marriages.

- Like her short stories, Lahiri's first novel, The Namesake (2003), deals with the experience of the second-generation Indian immigrant in the United States. Gogol Ganguli was born in the United States to Indian parents who had immigrated from Calcutta and settled in Cambridge, Massachusetts. But as he matures Gogol feels like an outsider, belonging neither to Indian nor American culture. The novel traces his painful attempts to discover his self-identity until he finally learns to accept both the American and the Indian aspects of his heritage.

- *The Middleman and Other Stories* (1988) is a collection of eleven stories by Indian-born American writer Bharati Mukherjee. She explores the immigrant experience in the United States, including that of not only Indians but also Italians, Filipinos, West Indians, and others. In the title story, an Iraqi Jew who is a recently naturalized American citizen finds himself working for a corrupt American rancher in a Central American country that is in the throes of a guerrilla insurgency. Mukherjee's stories document how immigration has changed the ethnic composition of the United States. They also examine the challenges faced by those who have recently arrived in an unfamiliar culture in which they are not always welcome.

- *Scent of Apples: A Collection of Stories,* by Filipino American writer Bienvenido Santos, was first published in 1979. Santos (1911–1996) wrote frequently about the experiences of Filipino immigrants to the United States. A typical story is "Immigration Blues," which examines the loneliness and sense of exile suffered by an old Filipino American widower who lives alone. He has been a US citizen since the end of World War II. Another story, "The Day the Dancers Came," shows how Filipino immigrants were often confined to low-status, low-wage jobs. *Scent of Apples* is available in a fifth edition published in 1997.

- *Immigration: The Ultimate Teen Guide* (2011), by Tatyana Kleyn, is a treasure trove of information and different perspectives regarding immigration in the United States. In twelve chapters, Kleyn, an immigrant herself, covers issues such as history and relevant terminology; statistical and demographic information; why people immigrate to the United States; undocumented immigration; refugees and those who have sought asylum; homesickness;language and cultural differences; discrimination; and laws and policies relating to immigration. Kleyn also discusses some of the myths regarding immigration and argues strongly against anti-immigrant sentiment. There are also many real-life stories of teens and young adults.

- In *Becoming American, Being Indian: An Immigrant Community in New York City* (2002), Madhulika S. Khandelwal describes the Indian immigrant community in New York City and how it has developed since it began in the 1960s. Drawing on interviews, Khandelwal examines how immigrants have preserved their own culture but have also been changed by their American experience.

- For those readers intrigued by the description of the Sun Temple at Konarak in "Interpreter of Maladies," *The Hindu Temple: An Introduction to Its Meaning and Forms,* by George Michell (1988), will be a fascinating book. Michell discusses the Konarak temple as well as numerous other examples of Hindu temples. The author explains the cultural, religious, and architectural significance of the temple, and the book includes numerous photographs.

Sources

Brada-Williams, Noelle, "Reading Jhumpa Lahiri's *Interpreter of Maladies* as a Short Story Cycle," in *MELUS*, Vol. 29, Nos. 3–4, Fall–Winter 2004, pp. 451–64.

Brians, Paul, "Jhumpa Lahiri: *Interpreter of Maladies* (2000)," in *Modern South Asian Literature in English*, Greenwood Press, 2003, p. 198.

"A Conversation with Jhumpa Lahiri," Houghton Mifflin Harcourt website, http://www.houghtonmifflinbooks.com/readers_guid (accessed July 31, 2012).

"The Indian American Community in the United States of America," Out of India, http://www.outofindia.net/abroad/WashingtonDC/in (accessed August 7, 2012).

"Indian-Americans: Demographic Information Updates," US India Political Action Committee (USINPAC) website, 2011, http://www.usinpac.com/indian-americans/demographic-info.html (accessed August 7, 2012).

Karim, Rezaul, "Jhumpa Lahiri," in *Dictionary of Literary Biography*, Vol. 323, *South Asian Writers in English*, edited by Fakrul Alam, Thomson Gale, 2006, pp. 205–10.

Lahiri, Jhumpa, "Interpreter of Maladies," in

Interpreter of Maladies: Stories, Houghton Mifflin, 1999, pp. 43–69. Shah, Purvi, Review of *Interpreter of Maladies,* in *Amerasia Journal,* Vol. 27, No. 2, 2001, pp. 183–86.

"Trading Stories: Notes from an Apprenticeship," in New Yorker, June 13, 2011, http://www.newyorker.com/reporting/2011/06/13/11 (accessed July 31, 2012).

Further Reading

Bala, Suman, ed., *Jhumpa Lahiri, the Master Storyteller: A Critical Response to "Interpreter of Maladies,"* Khosla Publishing House, 2002.

> This collection of essays offers a wide range of critical responses to Lahiri's stories.

Das, Nigamananda, ed., *Dynamics of Culture and Diaspora in Jhumpa Lahiri,* Adhyayan Publishers, 2010.

> This is a collection of eighteen essays by Indian scholars on all aspects of Lahiri's work. Of particular interest is the essay by Dipendu Das titled "Interpreting Maladies of the Exile: 'Interpreter of Maladies.'" Das explores the story in terms of the theme of exile.

Dhingra, Lavina, and Floyd Cheung, eds., *Naming Jhumpa Lahiri: Canons and Controversies,* Lexington Books, 2012.

> This is a collection of ten scholarly essays on Lahiri's work. In "Intimate Awakening: Jhumpa Lahiri, Diasporic Loss, and the Responsibility of the Interpreter," Rani Neutill employs psychoanalytic theory to analyze the story in terms

of how the characters deal with loss.

Srikanth, Rajini, *The World Next Door: South Asian American Literature and the Idea of America,* Temple University Press, 2004.

> This is a scholarly study of the contribution to American literature made by South Asian American writers from countries including Bangladesh, Pakistan, India, Sri Lanka, and Burma. Srikanth also offers a reading of Lahiri's "Interpreter of Maladies" (pp. 248–52).

Suggested Search Terms

Jhumpa Lahiri

Interpreter of Maladies

Konarak

Sun Temple

Surya

second-generation immigrants

immigration AND United States

Indian literature in English

South Asian American literature

CPSIA information can be obtained
at www.ICGtesting.com
Printed in the USA
BVHW041300150821
614465BV00017B/1665